MYSTERIO

BY AARON TREJO

BELLWETHER MEDIA • MINNEAPOLIS, MN

Are you ready to take it to the extreme?
Torque books thrust you into the action-packed world
of sports, vehicles, mystery, and adventure. These books
may include dirt, smoke, fire, and dangerous stunts.
WARNING : read at your own risk.

Library of Congress Cataloging-in-Publication Data

Trejo, Aaron.
Rey Mysterio / by Aaron Trejo.
    p. cm. -- (Torque: pro wrestling champions)
Includes bibliographical references and index.
Summary: "Engaging images accompany information about Rey Mysterio. The combination of
high-interest subject matter and light text is intended for students in grades 3 through 7"--Provided by
publisher.
ISBN 978-1-60014-639-8 (hardcover : alk. paper)
1. Rey Mysterio. 2. Wrestlers--United States--Biography. I. Title.
GV1196.R45T74 2011
796.812092--dc22

[B]   2011013158

CONTENTS

TRIPLE
THREAT
MATCH

Rey Mysterio entered the ring at WrestleMania 22. He was about to wrestle for the World Heavyweight Championship. It was a rare **Triple Threat Match** between Mysterio, Randy Orton, and current champion Kurt Angle. The first wrestler to pin either of his opponents would be the winner.

VITAL STATS

Wrestling Name: ------------ Rey Mysterio

Real Name: ------------ Óscar Gutiérrez

Height: --------- 5 feet, 6 inches (1.7 meters)

Weight: --------- 175 pounds (80 kilograms)

Started Wrestling: ---------------- 1989

Finishing Move: ------------------ 619

Each man survived several **near falls**. At one point, Angle had Mysterio in a painful **ankle lock**. Mysterio tried to **tap out**, but Orton distracted the referee. Then Mysterio threw Angle out of the ring. He turned and hit Orton with a powerful **619**. Mysterio climbed to the top rope and finished Orton off with a **West Coast Pop**. The referee counted to three. Mysterio was the new champion!

QUICK HIT!

Pinning Orton was a sweet victory for Mysterio. At the time, Orton was his biggest rival.

WHO IS REY MYSTERIO?

QUICK HIT!

As a kid, Gutiérrez was a skilled gymnast. This helped him develop his high-flying wrestling style.

Rey Mysterio's real name is Óscar Gutiérrez. He was born on December 11, 1974 in Chula Vista, California. When he was young, Gutiérrez watched **lucha libre** matches. His uncle was a famous Mexican *luchador*, or fighter, who competed as Rey Mysterio. Gutiérrez wanted to become a wrestler like his uncle.

Gutiérrez started training with his uncle around age 13. He was small, but he was a good athlete. He soon started taking part in lucha libre matches. He fought under the name *Colirbi*, which is Spanish for "hummingbird." Later, he fought as Rey Mysterio, Jr. and teamed up with his uncle.

Gutiérrez started wrestling full time in 1992. He and his friend Dionicio Castellanos Torres joined a Mexican wrestling league. Torres fought as Psicosis. The two carried on a bitter **feud** in the ring.

BECOMING A CHAMPION

In 1995, Mysterio and Psicosis joined a larger league called Extreme Championship Wrestling (ECW). They continued their feud there. Mysterio left ECW the following year to join World Championship Wrestling (WCW). He fought as a **cruiserweight** and won several championships.

QUICK HIT!

One of the matches between Mysterio and Psicosis was voted ECW's top match of 1995.

QUICK HIT!

Mysterio dropped the "Jr." from his name when he started wrestling for WWE.

WCW became part of WWE in 2001. Mysterio pinned Chavo Guerrero to win his first match. He quickly became a **face** and a fan favorite. He and Edge won the Tag Team Championship in 2002. Mysterio later won the WWE Cruiserweight Championship several times.

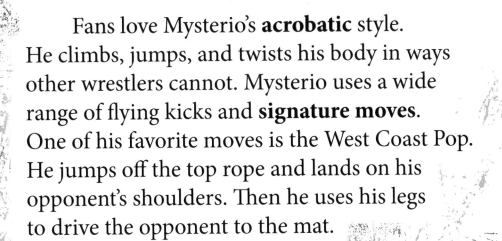

Fans love Mysterio's **acrobatic** style. He climbs, jumps, and twists his body in ways other wrestlers cannot. Mysterio uses a wide range of flying kicks and **signature moves**. One of his favorite moves is the West Coast Pop. He jumps off the top rope and lands on his opponent's shoulders. Then he uses his legs to drive the opponent to the mat.

QUICK HIT!

Mysterio fought The Big Show in one of his most famous matches. The Big Show stands 7 feet (2.1 meters) tall and weighs 485 pounds (220 kilograms).

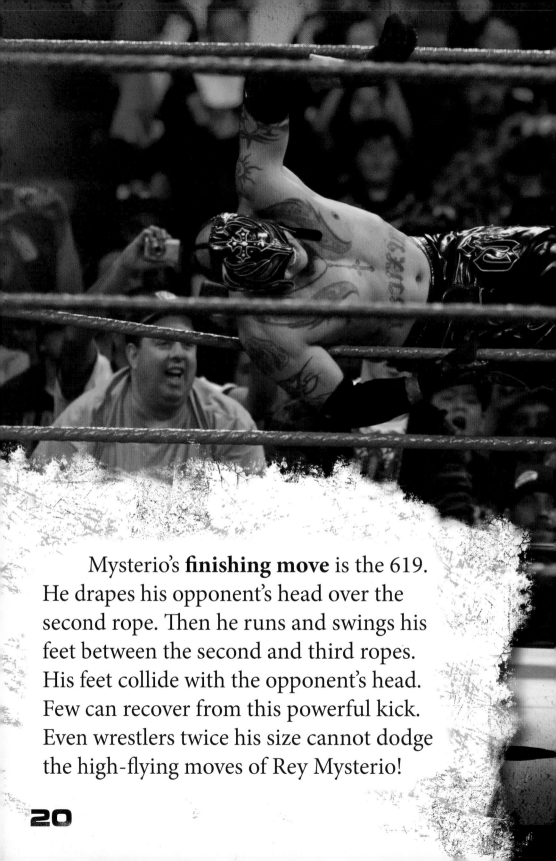

Mysterio's **finishing move** is the 619. He drapes his opponent's head over the second rope. Then he runs and swings his feet between the second and third ropes. His feet collide with the opponent's head. Few can recover from this powerful kick. Even wrestlers twice his size cannot dodge the high-flying moves of Rey Mysterio!

GLOSSARY

619—Rey Mysterio's finishing move; with his opponent's head between the second and third ropes, Mysterio runs, grabs both ropes, and swings his feet into the opponent's head.

acrobatic—having gymnastic balance and control

ankle lock—a submission hold in which a wrestler holds his opponent's leg and twists his ankle

cruiserweight—a wrestler who weighs 215 pounds (98 kilograms) or less

face—a wrestler seen by fans as a hero

feud—a long-lasting conflict between two people or teams

finishing move—a wrestling move meant to finish off an opponent so that he can be pinned

lucha libre—a style of Mexican wrestling known for masks and high-flying moves; *lucha libre* means "free wrestling" in Spanish.

near falls—pin attempts that fail just before the third count

signature moves—moves that a wrestler is famous for performing

tap out—to quit a match due to pain or injury caused by a submission hold

Triple Threat Match—a match in which three wrestlers fight at the same time; the first wrestler to pin either of his opponents wins the match.

West Coast Pop—a move in which a wrestler jumps onto the shoulders of his opponent and drives him to the mat

TO LEARN MORE

AT THE LIBRARY

Black, Jake. *The Ultimate Guide to WWE.* New York, N.Y.: Grosset & Dunlap, 2010.

Garza, Xavier. *Lucha Libre: The Man in the Silver Mask: A Bilingual Cuento.* El Paso, Tex.: Cinco Puntos Press, 2005.

Kaelberer, Angie Peterson. *Cool Pro Wrestling Facts.* Mankato, Minn.: Capstone Press, 2011.

ON THE WEB

Learning more about Rey Mysterio is as easy as 1, 2, 3.

1. Go to www.factsurfer.com.

2. Enter "Rey Mysterio" into the search box.

3. Click the "Surf" button and you will see a list of related Web sites.

With factsurfer.com, finding more information is just a click away.

INDEX